How to ~~Talk to~~
Anyone

*A Practical Guide to Avoid Anxiety,
Shyness, and Awkwardness. Make Real
Friends and Generate Deep
Conversations the Right and Simple Way*

Richard Hawkins

Furthermore, the transmission, duplication or reproduction of any of the following work including specific information will be considered an illegal act irrespective of if it is done electronically or in print. This extends to creating a secondary or tertiary copy of the work or a recorded copy and is only allowed with express written consent from the Publisher. All additional rights reserved.

The information in the following pages is broadly considered to be a truthful and accurate account of facts and as such any inattention, use or misuse of the information in question by the reader will render any resulting actions solely under their purview. There are no scenarios in which the publisher or the original author of this work can be in any fashion deemed liable for any hardship or damages that may befall them after undertaking information described herein.

Additionally, the information in the following pages is intended only for informational purposes and should thus be thought of as universal. As befitting its nature, it is presented without assurance regarding its prolonged validity or interim quality. Trademarks that are mentioned are done without written consent and can in no way be considered an endorsement from the trademark holder.

Table of Contents

Introduction

Congratulations on downloading this book and thank you for doing so.

The following chapters will discuss all of the pertinent information that you need to advance your communication skills to a more master level. You will start by exploring verbal communication, as well as the accompanying body language and other nonverbal elements. This is important because you need to master this form of communication before the others.

The next step will be looking at both digital and manual forms of written communication. You will get a chance to take your ability to do everything from writing emails to handwriting a memo to the next level.

Your visual and video communication abilities will be discussed next. Since technology is so important in today's world, these are two forms of communication that need to be mastered to become an advanced communicator.

You will be exposed to both group and one-on-one communication. While there are many similarities between the two concerning techniques, the differences are what you need to focus on to better advance your skills.

This book will go beyond just the communication type basics. You will explore formal vs. informal communication. You will learn when each is appropriate and the different subtypes that exist.

More advanced communication types and techniques are introduced. You will learn about expressive vs. receptive communication, as well as how to effectively communicate with those with specific challenges, such as having autism, or being visually or hearing impaired.

The final chapter explores conflict communication. There are very specific elements to consider when you need to communicate in an atmosphere where there might be hostility present.

There are plenty of books on this subject on the market, thanks again for choosing this one! Every effort was made to ensure it is full of as much useful information as possible. Please enjoy!

Chapter 1: Combining Verbal and Nonverbal Communication

Verbal communication is almost primal. It is at the very foundation of your daily life and you do it without even thinking about it. You say "hello" to friends and quickly provide an answer to a coworker's questions. This form of communication tells others a lot about you, especially concerning your technique. It typically includes both your words and the nonverbal clues that you give.

The nonverbal element of verbal communication is largely unconscious. For example, someone asks if you are okay. You are having a rough time, but you tell them that you are fine. Your body language can tell the other person that you are not being truthful and that something is wrong. Perhaps, you have a negative facial expression, or you do not look them in the eye when answering. This is why both verbal and nonverbal communication goes hand-in-hand.

Consider advertising to see the impact that verbal and nonverbal communication have when they are working together. You are at a mall and there is a booth set up to demonstrate the latest blender. The salesperson demonstrating the product is passionate, upbeat and really draws you in. Now, his words are what give you the merits of the blender, but his body language is what keeps you interested in what he is saying.

The example above describes a situation that you are exposed to on a daily basis. Consumers are constantly making purchasing decisions based more on the presenter than the product or service itself. How many things have you purchased in the last five years that just did not live up to the hype? Most people have at least one. Now, what made you think it was a good purchase decision initially? It ultimately comes down to the verbal and nonverbal communication utilized by the person telling you about the product.

Body Language in Verbal Communication

Like you learned above, body language is almost like a natural and unconscious lie detector. You can tell a friend that you are fine when they ask, but if your body language says otherwise, they know that you are not being truthful with them.

The next time you are considering a product or service based on advertising, consider the nonverbal cues. In this industry, the following are used to persuade consumers to make a purchase:

- Showing people where to look
- Using eyes to make a stronger point
- Pointing to the most attractive element
- Smiling to convey a sense of the product or service causing happiness
- Using the right colors to persuade
- Using dollar amounts to convey a feeling of greater value

Now that you know what these persuasive nonverbal cues are, it is time to start using them in all of your verbal communications. This might seem manipulative, but it is not. Instead, use your body language to strengthen the point that you are trying to make. This is helpful in all areas, but especially when you are at work.

For example, you are up for a promotion and three other coworkers are also being considered. What you say during your interview must match your body language to convince the interviewer that you are truly the best candidate for the promotion. You want to combine your verbal and nonverbal communication to create an atmosphere that is warm and humble, but also exciting. In this type of situation, you are essentially selling yourself so using tried and true advertising techniques will be your most effective communication tool.

Verbal Communication Skills to Master

Certain communication skills may appear basic on the surface but mastering them will make you the most advanced communicator possible. The following are the skills you want to focus on:

- Make sure that you are friendly and approachable. This automatically makes people more open to hearing what you have to say. It also gives you a chance to provide some feel-good vibes to those who you are speaking with.

- Before you speak, take a few seconds to consider what you will say. You have certainly heard sayings that state that silence can be your best answer. This is true. There are times when not saying anything is the best way to communicate. If a verbal response is warranted, you want to ensure that it is received in the way that you intend it to be. A quick second to think will help to ensure this.

- Always be clear when you speak. Do not beat around the bush, per se. Get your thoughts out in the open, but do so in a way that is constructive and articulate. This is a skill that takes some practice and may require a little thinking on your part. Remember that communication should be smooth, and people should not have to ask what you mean when you make a statement. It should be immediately clear.

- Know when to talk and when to listen. All humans have a trace of narcissism. A little bit is actually a good thing and it is natural. However, this can also negatively impact your ability to effectively communicate. When you are speaking with a group or an individual, know when it is appropriate to talk.

- Always make sure that you are authentic and true. If you are not, those you are talking to will pick up on this. Ensure all of your words are transparent and that your nonverbal communication matches your words.

- Work on your humility. As stated above, a little narcissism is natural and not a bad thing. However, you cannot sacrifice respect for others due to it. People will be able to tell if you are really hearing what they have to say and truly listening.

- When you talk, do so with confidence. Balancing humility and confidence is a skill that you will need to work on because it does not come naturally to most people. However, once you strike the balance, your verbal communication skills will automatically be boosted.

- Be mindful of your body language. Remember that this is largely unconscious, but it is possible to be able to recognize it. You want to be able to see what others see concerning the unspoken elements of your communication.

- Always be concise and stick to $10 words over $1,000 ones. This means that you want to use vocabulary that applies to the widest audience possible. This is critical to ensuring that everyone you speak to receive the message the way you intend it.

- Always listen to others and do so in a way that is genuine. This is where your active listening skills come into play. This is another advanced communication technique that takes time to master, but it is imperative.

Start by evaluating these individually. All of them are equally important and it is imperative that you can get all of them to an advanced level. As you master one, come back to this list and go to the next. Even just mastering one of these will allow you to be more effective no matter the situation in which you are utilizing verbal communication.

Verbal Modeling

The most effective communicators are experts in verbal modeling. It is human nature to want to be around people who are similar to you. This is why people often choose their friends based on similar interests and lifestyles. This is essentially a law of human nature and you can take full advantage of it to enhance your communication skills. Verbal modeling is essentially a method in which you match the modulation and voice tone of those you are communicating with.

For example, if the person you are talking to tends to speak softly, you too should speak softly. People are more receptive to those who speak like they do. When you master verbal modeling, you will find that your relationships are more meaningful, your self-esteem is improved, and your market value is increased.

Exercising Your Verbal Communication Skills

One of the most effective ways to exercise your skills is to ask for feedback. Consider those you communicate with on a regular basis. Ask them to provide some constructive criticism.

Do you get your message across clearly? Are you an authentic communicator? When they are talking, does it appear that you are truly listening to them? Just keep an open mind when you are getting the answers to these questions. Remember that some people might be harsher than others when evaluating you, but this is a good thing. It gives you the best information to start your own personal evaluation.

The second way to exercise your skills is to talk to yourself. For this, a full-length mirror is best. Just talk about something that you are knowledgeable about in front of a mirror. Make sure to keep eye contact with yourself. Did you appear comfortable? Did you appear trustworthy and did you get your message across with brevity and clarity? You might also consider talking to yourself via video so that you can go back and watch it. Take notes about what needs to change to make your verbal communication more effective. Also, make sure that you pay special attention to your nonverbal communication as you do this. Does it match what you are saying?

You can see that while verbal communication is so basic, it can be your greatest asset once you master it. It allows you to get more of what you want, and it has a major impact on your overall productivity. Just remember that improving this element of communication requires intentional effort, constant awareness and the desire to get better.

Chapter 2: Digital Written Communication

In the last week, you have surely written an email, conversed on social media, or posted on a digital message board. All of these are forms of digital written communication. While people do still put pen to paper, it is largely becoming extinct in favor of digital methods.

The one element of digital communication that is most difficult is getting your true message across with ease. There is no body language, tone of voice or other telling elements like you have when speaking to a person face-to-face.

One of the most difficult parts of digital communication is remembering to be concise. Since you have to convey your message purely via text, it is easy to essentially overexplain yourself. You want to remember the rules of verbal communication concerning clarity and brevity since they apply here too. Avoid descriptors and fluff in your digital communications. However, you have to also be mindful of your verbiage so that your digital messages do not come across as harsh and cold.

Email Communication

When you want to look at how to improve your email communication skills to an advanced level, look at some of the most effective email marketing campaigns. The message, first and foremost, must have value and the overall intention must be clear starting with the headline. People choose whether or not to open an email based on the subject line. The subject line can also determine whether an email is easily visible or sent to the spam folder based on the email carrier's algorithm.

Birchbox email marketing is a good example of how to properly communicate via email. The headline is enticing, but at the same time, it gets to the point. Now, once recipients open the email, they are greeted personally. All good email communication will be personalized with the recipient's name. Yes, this can take a few extra minutes if you need to send the same message to multiple people, but this extra step automatically makes the recipient feel special. When people feel special, they are more likely to not only read the entire email, but they are also more likely to interpret it in a positive way.

Next, Birchbox got right to the point in the first sentence. They avoided flowery language and told recipients exactly what these needed to know. The message was broken up into short sentences and paragraphs, ensuring that it was easy to read. The final sentence was positive and upbeat.

These techniques work for every email that you are sending. It is important that after reading, your recipient feels positive. This is especially critical if the content of the email is offering bad news or constructive criticism.

No matter the intention behind your email or the type of content, keep the following in mind:

- Ensure that the subject line accurately reflects the content and is meaningful
- Do not use attachments unless absolutely necessary
- Address the recipients by name to add personalization
- Always be kind and avoid words and phrases that flame

- Never assume privacy, so avoid adding any confidential information
- When you are sent a response or an initial message, always respond promptly
- Make sure that the message stays on track and focused
- Clearly identify yourself from the start
- Always proofread before sending
- Make sure to make the distinction between informal and formal situations
- Show restraint and respect, especially when the email is on a tough subject

Text Message Communication

Texting used to be a way for friends to send a quick message to each other. However, in today's world, it is used for all forms of communication, including in a professional environment. Because of this, it must be used properly to be effective. It is a good idea to get into the habit of texting all people in the same manner. Keep it professional, do not use shorthand and use the least words possible. Make sure that your punctuation and grammar are also clean.

If you are linking to a website via a text message, use shortened links so that the message is clean and not overwhelmed by the link. This is a form of text message etiquette that will be appreciated by every person you are communicating with. Think about the last time you go an advertisement via text message. The message itself was no more than two sentences and the language was direct.

Any links were shortened so that the message itself was the focus.

When you are communicating via text message and need it to be professional, there are some tips that you can use. A few of these are relatively basic, but most allow you to advance your skills. Start with mastering the few that are basic and then move onto the next. These tips include:

- Keep the message short without sacrificing the message and tone
- Personalize the message so that the recipient knows that you are taking their needs into consideration
- Make sure the content of the message is high in quality and restrict the frequency to only when necessary

- When you are replying to a text message, avoid using a single word. Using just one word can make the person who sent the text feel as though you do not value what they had to say

- If your message contains more than one option, sum them up in the shortest way possible and make sure that there is a clear break between the different options offered

- Most of all, make sure that all of your messages have value and a purpose. Even if the purpose is just checking in, it should be meaningful

Social Media Communication

Just about everyone in the modern world has at least one social media account. Social media platforms, such as Facebook, Instagram, and Twitter make it easier to keep up with loved ones, meet new people, stay on top of the latest news and even advertise. In fact, the social media platform LinkedIn is the most widely used for connecting like-minded professionals. Just like with texting, when it comes to social media communication you want to be consistent. Stick with a professional and authentic tone. Ensure proper spelling and grammar, avoid shorthand and perfect your punctuation. Proofread your posts and comments before posting them and keep them brief and to the point.

Taking a look at social media marketing is a good way to familiarize yourself with some of the more advanced communication techniques on this type of platform. This form of marketing essentially uses social media to share news about a company or to promote products and services. The fact that it is efficiently interactive draws people to it naturally.

By using the same strategies that successful social media marketers use, you can take your communication game on this type of platform to a more advanced level. These techniques include:

- Plan out your posts so that they are relevant and most likely to spark interest

- Use visual enhancers, such as photos, to catch the attention of friends and followers

- Interact with those who leave comments to encourage conversation and an exchange of ideas

- Get personal, but not overly so, to ensure that your friends and followers can connect with your human side and better see the origins of your perspective

- Utilize hashtags and other techniques to ensure that your posts and content are easy to find

- Be clear about why you are saying or sharing something

- Ask open-ended questions to encourage sharing and discussion

- Tell a story, but make sure that it is engaging while also being short and concise

- Remember that quality is more important than how much you post

- Ensure that your content is original. Repetition and seeing the same topics frequently will reduce engagement and the opportunity to communicate with others

- Really listen to the comments and feedback that you receive and respond appropriately

From here, the best way to improve your social media communication abilities is to constantly evaluate. Are you getting more meaningful interaction with your friends and followers? This is a good way to measure how much your skills are improving.

Website Communication

Whether you have a personal website or blog, or you manage any of these for your employer, how you present the content will determine how successfully it is received. In today's world, more and more people are turning to blogs and websites to get information. This means that most companies have some form of blog or website. You must keep the brand in mind and ensure that every person who reads the content views it as you intended.

Forbes is considered to be one of the most widely read websites on the internet. Every month, they get an estimated 65,000,000 unique visitors. While the subjects they present do play a role in this, the quality of the content and how it is communicated is what keeps people coming back and sharing the content on social media and via other digital avenues.

When you are communicating via a website or blog, you have to keep in mind that the audience will always be incredibly diverse. Your readers will be people from all backgrounds, multiple education levels and likely from different areas of the world. Every word you write has to keep these facts in mind. When you are creating this type of content, the following communication tips help to ensure that what you produce is relevant to the largest audience possible:

- Communicate with your readers as you would your friends

- Make sure that the most important message is stated first since internet readers have a short attention span

- Avoid being too creative and clever. Deliver the communication clearly and with brevity

- Make sure to keep scanners in mind. These are people who quickly scan the content looking for the information that they seek. Use subheads, bullet points and other methods to break up the content and make it easier to digest

- Use words that are familiar. Avoid extensive vocabulary and industry jargon

- Ensure the website is easy to navigate

- Add in visual elements, such as photos

With each piece, the following writing tips will help to ensure that your message is communicated properly and in a way that encourages people to read it:

- Keep paragraphs to no more than four sentences

- Keep sentences to no more than 12 words

- Avoid needless repetition

- Keep your text as tight and short as possible without sacrificing pertinent information

- Skip unnecessary words

- Limit or avoid using past tense

- Directly address your visitors by writing in second person

Chapter 3: Manual Written Communication

You probably remember the days where you would pass notes to your friends in class, write your pen pal or send handwritten cards or invitations. While digital communication makes these tasks faster and easier, it is still important to be able to effectively communicate via manual writing. You never know when taking a pen to paper will allow you to convey your message in the most effective way possible.

Throughout your time in school, you wrote papers and completed similar assignments. The purpose was to prove your knowledge of the subject matter and to ensure your written communication skills were satisfactory. Just like with digital written communication, manual writing comes with some challenges. There is no tone of voice, body language or the ability to gauge the interest of your reader. You simply have to allow your written communication style to tackle all of this.

While digital communication is more common today, you still use manual writing too. For example, you might need to take notes in class or in a work meeting, write quick memos or leave instructions for a family member to tackle a chore, such as how to prepare a quick meal. Your writing must be easy to understand, concise and you must also make your mood clear via your written words.

The following are areas where you want to focus whenever you engage in manual written communication:

- Keep your sentences short and try not to exceed 14 words per sentence
- Make sure that your handwriting is neat and easy to read. If you tend to write larger, consider double-spacing so that words do not connect and take on a jumbled appearance
- Use black or blue ink and paper that is white and plain for professional correspondence
- Use simple language
- Put the most pertinent information up top so that you can be sure that it is seen
- Always be succinct

- Utilize active voice whenever possible and only use passive when using this voice allows for greater clarity
- Separate ideas and make the separation clear
- Personalize your communication by addressing the recipient by name

Manual writing takes a bit longer and there is no backspace to get rid of mistakes. Because of this, you want to ensure that you take your time and it is a good idea to outline the communication and complete the organization before grabbing your pen.

Think back to when you were in school and working on a major report. Your teacher likely had you create an outline first so that you could identify the key points and structure it in a way that allowed the differing ideas to flow into one another. This was done to make your life easier once you got started with the writing process. Brainstorming and making sure that you know what needs to be written beforehand eliminates the need to scrap your draft and start over.

Just like with all forms of writing, you must consider your audience. With friends and family, you can get away with being a bit more lax with structure and content. However, you must still ensure that you articulate your points. Again, remember that your words must not only deliver the right information, but also the tone you are intending.

With manual writing, avoid acronyms unless you know that your recipient knows exactly what they are. It is best to just write out the total phrase to avoid confusion otherwise.

Make sure that you do not go off on tangents when using this form of communication. This can distract from your message and make it harder to understand what you are trying to say.

The good news is that anyone can become a more effective communicator in the written form. However, this will not happen overnight. Consider your favorite writer and how they keep you interested and engaged. You essentially need to find your own style while making sure that your style is one that is direct and easy to understand and interpret. Once you master the advanced techniques of this form of written communication, you can parlay it into all forms of communication to become more skillful.

With this information, you can start working on your manual written communication. Practice is the best way to make sure that you master the most advanced techniques. When appropriate, skip digital writing and use manual. For example, send out birthday cards instead of using social media to offer birthday wishes. You might also consider writing short memos at work instead of sending them via email.

Chapter 4: Visual or Video Communication

Visual and video communication are different but similar, so it makes sense to discuss them together. Visual communication uses visual means, such as images, to entertain, enlighten, persuade and inform an audience. Think back to when you were in school and you used posters and slideshows when giving a presentation. This is a type of visual communication. From an advertising perspective, billboards and signage are types of visual communication. Video communication is essentially verbal communication delivered via video. Think of Skype or a television commercial as examples of video communication.

Visual Communication

As stated above, this is a way to communicate using visual means. What was the last billboard that you saw? What about this billboard made you notice it? Billboards are a type of outdoor advertising, so there are multiple elements in the general vicinity that can catch your attention. Why did the billboard get your attention ahead of everything else? These answers to these questions are what you need to become an effective visual communicator.

To get started, take a few minutes to explore what the experts consider the best techniques to make a billboard an effective advertising tool:

- Use six words or less for this element of the communication. Experts in billboard advertising state that most people only read the first six words

- Create the visual in a way that is not distracting, but also easy to notice

- Do not utilize direct response measures with this form of communication. This is not an ideal way to encourage a response, but to make something or a bit of information known

- Avoid being overly clever, but ensure that the visual leaves a lasting impression

- Balance the number of visual used to get the point across without creating clutter

- Show your message more than you say it. This is where you would decide to incorporate relevant features, such as moving parts or 3D elements

- Make sure that your visual does not have any repetition

- Always keep it simple. Visuals are meant to be read and understood within seconds by people of all backgrounds

- If there is some type of logo present, it should be visible, but never dominate the visual

- Ensure that the visual can be seen by everyone. For example, if you are doing a presentation in class, the people in the front row and back row should all be able to see it easily

Now, where does visual communication fit into daily life? You are already using it. For example, you and your family are planning a vacation. You present brochures of the destinations that you are considering. These brochures are the visual communication. You also use it when you give presentations and work or school, or even when you post a meme on social media. This is a form of communication that is present in all areas of your life. Mastering it will make it much easier for you to convey the right message.

For example, you are talking to friends about a new restaurant you want to take them to. You would pull up photos of the restaurant itself, the cuisine and different social media photos that past guests have posted. Or, you are discussing something like vaccines with someone. You might pull up statistical graphs and charts to back your point. Once you master visual communication, it will stand alone, and you will need little to no verbal communication to back up your points and opinions.

Just like with verbal and written communication, your visuals should be concise and to the point. They must be authentic and accurate. They should also be easy to understand.

Video Communication

In today's world where technology is at the foundation of most interaction, you will eventually use video to communicate if you do not already. People use platforms, such as Skype, to chat with friends and loved ones, especially when they do not live close to each other. This makes it possible to have face-to-face conversations. In the professional world, video conferencing is a very popular way for people all over the world to have a meeting at the same time.

Looking at personal communications via video, you would approach this in mostly the same way that you do face-to-face verbal communication. Just ensure proper lighting and for at least the top half of your body to be visible. This ensures that the person you are communicating with can see your body language as you speak.

When you are talking to a friend or other loved one via video, time is often short. Because of this, you want to front-load your conversation with what is most important. When you know that you will be communicating with someone via video, consider jotting down a few quick points that you want to ensure to discuss. Keep this list with you so that you do not forget. This can also improve the flow of the conversation.

Another element of communicating via video is making sure that you are not interrupting the other person. If you have used this platform for communication, you know that it can be easier to interject due to the person not physically being present. While you are conversing, you are still in the room alone, so you put yourself first. This is unconscious and natural. As you work on advancing your video communication skills, this is the first place to start.

Some recommend that you visualize the person physically sitting in front of you. Make sure that you both are using similar lighting and a similar tone and volume of your voices. This can make the setting feel a little more intimate and more intimate settings put you on a more level playing field, per se.

While chatting via video can feel a bit artificial, it is important that you do not let this impact the quality of the conversation. Make sure that you communicate with the person as you would normally when you see them in person. Ensure that you are relaxed, and even when short on time, do not rush the conversation. As long as you articulate properly and go into the conversation with a purpose, this will start to become natural as your communication skills using this platform grow stronger.

The next common use for video communication is for business purposes. Major corporations throughout the world utilize video conferencing to make meetings more efficient. Gone are the days where you must travel to different locations and meet people separately. This ensures that all participants are getting the same information and that every person can provide and receive feedback with ease.

There are certain communication etiquette points to consider when doing business communication via video conferencing:

- It is important that you do an audio check beforehand. Use microphones and speakers that are clear and crisp

- When you are talking, annunciate your words and speak slowly, but naturally

- When you are speaking, use eye contact with those on the screen just as you would at a meeting in person

- Pay attention to the body language of those on the screen because this lets you know if you are being both heard and understood

- As long as you have quality audio equipment, there is no need to raise your voice to ensure that you are heard. If you start to shout or speak louder than usual, this can make you appear aggressive and you can lose the attention of those you are speaking to

- Keep your movements in check. Allow your natural body language to occur, but avoid excessive jerking, position changes, talking with your hands or moving your head around

- When other people are talking, do not interrupt them. Instead, use the same active listening techniques you use when talking to people in person

- The person speaking should have your undivided attention. Never carry on a side conversation throughout the video conference

- Make sure that you are dressed professionally. Even if you are doing the conference from your home office, dress as you would when going into the office. You should also avoid wearing clothing that is too vibrant, that blends into the background or that is otherwise visually distracting

- Be yourself and make sure that you interact with those on video as you do with those you are communicating with in person. Authenticity will be just as obvious via video communication

Chapter 5: Communicating with a Language Barrier

Being able to speak more than one language fluently is an invaluable communication skill. However, even if you just speak one language, you can still master being able to interact with people from all cultures and languages. This is very important in all areas of life, but especially in the workplace. If you work for a company that has contacts and clients all over the world, when you can deliver the same message to all people, you become more valuable. This can aid you in getting promotions and being afforded greater responsibility.

On a personal level, this type of skill will allow you to expand your horizons concerning the people you can develop relationships with. It also makes it easier to travel. When you can effectively communicate despite a language barrier, you will be able to more fully immerse yourself in the place you are visiting. You will learn more about the area and be able to take advantage of more exciting opportunities.

Now, when you are not fluent, there will be some obvious challenges concerning interacting with those who speak a different language. However, with the right approach and information, you can still communicate with each other, at least to convey and understand basic needs and facts. Consider the following when working to master this type of communication:

- Start by working on understanding one culture and communication style at a time. This will make it much easier compared to going back and forth and trying to remember which fact is assigned to which culture.

- Make sure that you know the name of the language spoken by the culture that you are learning more about. From here, you should strive to learn at least a few basic phrases associated with the language. Be aware that certain countries have more than one language. Because of this, you will have to know the region of the person you are interacting with. For example, there are 11 official languages in South Africa and four official languages in Singapore. This will be helpful whether you are traveling or interacting with people in a professional capacity.

- Survey those you know who are familiar with the culture or language that you are studying. Just be sure to always double check any facts that they might give you to ensure accuracy.

- When it is imperative that information be completely accurate and delivered precisely, consider working with an interpreter. There are freelance interpreters that you can use as needed so there is no need to utilize them full-time. If you find one that is not local, you can always take advantage of their services via video conferencing.

- Take written communication and translate it. For example, Google

Translate is a free service for smaller forms of written communication. However, keep in mind that this might not always be fully accurate. This is a way to get a general idea. You should utilize professional translation services where there is no room for error.

- Take advantage of technology when it is appropriate. There are software and even mobile apps that will help you to learn basic phrases, get common cultural facts and even do some basic translations for you.

- Visual communication tends to be far more universal than written and verbal. A photo of a balloon is a balloon no matter the background or language of the person you are communicating with, for example. Just ensure that your visual aids are precise, clear and respectful of the other culture you are seeking to interact with.

- Keep your communication simple. For example, do not use jargon, idioms or slang. This can be perceived much differently than you intend it to be, resulting in confusion. You could also unintentionally offend the person you are trying to communicate with.

- Do not be afraid to ask for clarification. Remember that when you are communicating with someone and there is a language barrier, the barrier is present for them as well. Frequently ensuring that you are properly understanding without having a condescending tone will be appreciated.

- Take the time to ensure all team members are on the same page. If you will be working with someone as a group, all members should approach the situation in the same way and learn the same language and cultural basics.

This type of advanced communication skill is certainly one that will take work and practice. The best way to master it is to throw yourself into situations where you need to effectively communicate with people who speak a different language or follow a different culture. Remember that you must mind the cultural norms while communicating for the most productive experience.

Chapter 6: One-on-One Communication

This is a type of communication that you will find yourself in most often. You will speak to loved ones, coworkers, superiors and even strangers on a one-on-one basis regularly. If you expect to become a leader, this communication setting is one that you must master, and you need to do so with all forms of communication.

When speaking to someone alone, what you say and how you listen are equally important. You need to be able to grab their attention with your first sentence and then maintain it. You can use a classic marketing formula that is often used in advertorial copywriting for this:

- Attention
- Interest
- Desire
- Action

Getting attention can be achieved via all routes of communication. With verbal, you must ensure that your body language and words are matching. You must also engage in active listening. For the interest part of the equation, once you hook the other person, you have to hold their interest. From here, you must make them feel your desires as deeply as you do. This is one that will usually take more time to master than the other three. You have to be able to make them feel your desire without using any form of manipulation. Essentially, your passion should be enough, so you have to convey it in a neutral, factual and powerful way. Lastly, you need to be able to persuade them to take action. This is easiest in written communication because you can use the old marketing technique referred to as writing a call to action.

When you are talking to someone one-on-one, you need to essentially be able to discuss anything with them freely and with ease, but also while staying on point and getting the facts out there. This might sound contradictory, but once you master this communication method, you will see that the elements truly complement each other. Consider the following to have a productive and relaxing conversation one-on-one:

- Pay attention to the person's body language to determine how they are hearing what you are saying

- When you are listening, frequently reflect to make sure that you truly hear their points

- Monitor their behavior throughout the interaction

- Never judge without first getting all of the facts

- Know that there will not always be a mutual agreement, depending on the topic you are discussing

- Make it a point to learn at least one thing from every one-on-one conversation

- Keep the conversation neutral unless the situation calls for bias or personal anecdotes

- Know when silence is the better answer

These work for all forms of communication and not just verbal. The one exception would be during written communication, there is no body language to observe.

Active Listening

Half of communication is listening to the person you are interacting with. You need to not only hear or read their words, but you also need to make sure you understand them. Active listening is considered to be a type of advanced communication skill. This is because you are not born just being going at it. In fact, if you were not currently trying to advance your communication abilities, you might not have even heard of it. While it takes time to master, at its core, it is not difficult. The following describes the elements of active listening:

- Always maintain eye contact when you are listening and ensure that you are both facing each other

- Make sure that you are relaxed, but at the same time, it should be clear that they have your full attention

- Make sure that your mind is open to everything that they are saying

- Try to picture the situation being painted by the speaker to truly hear their words and perspective

- Never interrupt at any time when they are talking

- Asking questions to clarify is good, but only do this when the speaker takes a pause

- If you are unsure about something, ask questions, but avoid asking unnecessary questions

- Try to empathize with the speaker and see the source of their feelings and thoughts

- Provide feedback as they speak, but do so in a way that is not distracting or interrupting them

- Pay attention to their body language and nonverbal cues

Have you ever been pitched a product or service? It was just you and the marketer attempting to make a sale. When you asked questions, what were they doing? As long as they were skilled communicators, they were listening. They would essentially give the question back to you to show they heard you, and then they would answer it. When they were talking, they did so with conviction and authenticity. This is what you need to do during all one-on-one interactions.

Remember that all one-on-one communications are give and take. As you continue to develop your more advanced skills, you will be able to determine about exactly when to talk and when to listen. This will take time and practice.

Chapter 7: Group Communication

Group communication is very common. You might have meetings at work, lecture classes or even spend time with groups of friends or relatives. All of these situations call for your group communication skills to be superior. This is more challenging than one-on-one communication for a number of reasons. You have to take the thoughts and feelings of all people into consideration when you speak. You must also ensure that you give equal attention to all speakers via active listening. Of course, when you are speaking, you must ensure that you are engaging all members of the group. This probably sounds a bit overwhelming and it certainly can be at first. However, once you learn the advanced techniques associated with group communication, you will see that this is not only easy, but a great way to learn and exchange ideas.

Have you ever been a part of a focus group? This is a form of marketing that allows companies and inventors to get valuable and unbiased feedback on their products or services. By learning a bit more about focus groups and their general etiquette, you can better develop your group communication skills for a formal environment, such as in the workplace. The etiquette includes:

- Designate a moderator that will help to keep all participants on track

- Ensure that there is enough time for all participants to speak for the same amount of time, and allot a little extra time for unexpected interruptions

- Introduce the topic and basic facts associated with what will be discussed

- Set some ground rules concerning what is expected out of each participant

- For a professional group discussion, consider recording it for future reference, but make sure all participants know that they are being recorded

These tips also work for debate groups, groups discussing specific topics or even when a group of friends is discussing which activity they want to do together.

Talking in a Group Setting

It is imperative that all members of the group feel that they are being given equal attention and time to talk. You should also remember that speaking to a group might be a bit intimidating for those who tend to be shy or introverted, so make sure to empathize and keep this in mind. If you happen to be the nervous one, do not be afraid to state this upfront. Then, if there is a disconnection between your words and your body language, this can help to explain it so that you do not come off as not being authentic or knowledgeable.

There are a number of tips you can employ when speaking to a group. No matter your comfort level, these will help you to get through what you need to say far easier:

- If you make a mistake, just own it. This might even be a good time to inject a bit of humor, depending on the subject matter

- Know your audience by doing a bit of research before you are set to speak to a group

- Try to go under your allotted time by two to five minutes, depending on how much time you are being given

- Take advantage of incorporating different forms of visual communication as appropriate

- Do not be afraid to repeat key facts and phrases so that you can reinforce their importance

- If you are giving a group speech, make sure that you practice it beforehand

- Use pauses wisely and avoid saying things, such as "ummm" as much as possible

- Be direct and be confident in the facts that you are delivering

- When speaking to a group, spread your eye contact, but do so in a controlled way so it does not appear as though your attention is darting around the room

- Make it personal as appropriate with quick stories or comparisons that drive your point home

Listening in a Group Setting

For the most part, the active listening tips you learned in the previous chapter apply here and will be used in the exact same way. Do not interrupt, wait for a pause to ask for clarification, use eye contact, analyze their behavior and body language and ensure that they have your undivided attention. When in a group, there are often opportunities to break off into multiple discussions at the same time. While in a very casual environment, such as a group of friends at a bar, this can be appropriate, it is not in most circumstances.

In a professional group communication, consider taking notes. This will make it easier for you to get clarification at the end. In many work meetings, for example, all members are allowed to speak and provide their individual bits of information. Then, once it is all out on the table, questions are taken. In this type of situation, writing notes makes it easier to remember what you wanted to ask, why and the person you need to direct the questions to.

Lastly, whether you are listening or talking, consider the environment and the group dynamics. This will play a major role in how the discussion flows, whether formal or informal communication is needed and how to approach clarification or potentially negative thoughts and facts.

Chapter 8: Expressive and Receptive Communication

This is a form of communication you use often, but you likely do not even realize it. Essentially, this involves sending a person a message with the purpose to stop something or make something happen. To best understand this type of communication, you also need to know about the receptive type. When comparing the two, receptive is the ability to understand communication and expressive is the ability to communicate effectively. Both of these involve all forms of communication, ranging from verbal to visual, as well as specialty types of communication, such as sign language.

Mastering expressive and receptive communication is advanced in itself. Normal everyday people will not utilize these regularly. Because of this, you want to ensure that you master the communication types in all of the previous chapters before attempting these.

While mastering these is critical for having advanced communication skills, it is also necessary if you wish to effectively communicate with those who have altered communication abilities. For example, communicating well with those who have autism, those who are hearing impaired and those with visual impairment will require effective expressive and receptive communication skills.

Those with issues impacting their ability to communicate often require special attention to make sure that they can understand communication and express themselves appropriately. For example, when a person is hearing impaired, sign language makes it possible for them to best communicate since verbal communication may be difficult to impossible, depending on their level of hearing impairment and overall function.

Knowing how to effectively communicate those with language and communication impairments ensures that your message is properly conveyed. It also makes sure that you can understand the message they are trying to deliver to you. Exploring the communication techniques used when interacting with those with autism and those who are either hearing or visually impaired is the best place to start. Since this type of communication is not something people engage in daily, it tends to be a gradual learning process before you can master it.

Autism

There are varying severity levels of autism. A person's language development may take longer to develop, or it may be uneven. The person may either have reduced nonverbal skills or the inability to understand nonverbal cues. In some cases, those with autism do not use verbal communication. Due to the challenges, when you are communicating with a person who has autism, it is imperative that you do so in a way that they can best understand.

In addition to being yourself and ensuring that you are authentic, consider the following when communicating with a person who has autism:

- Keep the individual's specific communication challenges in mind during a conversation and be patient

- If they misunderstand what you are saying, patiently expand on your point

- Know that those with autism tend to not read between the lines and they take things literally. If you have watched the television show, "The Good Doctor," you have seen this. Dr. Shaun Murphy is autistic, and he often says things very pointedly and takes what other people say at face value. This can result in them asking frequent questions. Simply answer them. The person just wants to ensure that they understand what you are saying

- Do not get offended by their very honest and frank communication style. On the surface, it might appear rude, but this is not their intent

- Make eye contact, but do not expect it to be given

- Know that there could be insecurity present, so you must be authentic or else this will be picked up on

- Use a neutral volume and tone of voice

- Do not assume that the person lacks emotion or empathy just because it is not very noticeable

- Do not touch the person without first warning them

- Treat them as an equal and never be condescending

Hearing Impaired

Technology has helped to make communicating with the hearing impaired a bit easier. Televisions have subtitles and there are gadgets that can essentially translate verbal communication into written. You might also apt to advance your communication skills even further and learn sign language. Know the following for more advanced skills:

- Never yell or talk loudly. This can cause your body language to give inaccurate cues

- Speak at a neutral rate and avoid rapid or severely slowed speech

- Consider incorporating visual aids and written communication into the interaction

- Eliminate as much background noise as possible

- Never mumble and make sure that you annunciate your words

- When speaking, always make eye contact and ensure that you are both face-to-face

- Make sure that you are relaxed and be patient with them

- Ask the person for advice about how to make communication as smooth and efficient as possible

In a group setting where one or more hearing-impaired people are present, there are a few ways to enhance the communication among all participants. Create an itinerary for the group when this is possible. You can also use visual aids to help convey the most important information. When you are arranging the seating, make it so that all members of the group can clearly see each other. Lastly, have all participants raise their hands before speaking so that the entire group knows who to focus on, make sure the environment is quiet and ensure that only a single person talks at a time.

Visually Impaired

Brail and devices that translate written communication into verbal communication have made it easier for communication between those who are visually impaired and those who are not a bit more efficient. However, there is further information to know to ensure that your ability to communicate with a visually impaired person is as advanced and understandable as possible. This includes:

- First and foremost, make your presence known by identifying who you are. You should also personalize your introduction. For example, "hi, Sam, it is Laura."

- Do not attempt to suppress your body language because this will have a negative impact on your tone of voice

- Never use third person when talking

- Make it clear when the conversation has ended, and you are leaving

- Try to communicate in a quiet environment

- Always relax and act as you do when communicating with all people

- Speak clearly and naturally, and still use eye contact

- Utilize everyday language

- Introduce all people in the group when there is more than one person present

- If you are giving direction, make sure that your language is specific and accurate

- Ask if they have a preferred communication method or if help is needed

Whether you regularly interact with those who have special communication needs or not, it is ideal to still work on your skills. This will ensure that you are prepared should the situation present itself. Also, when you are working to master more advanced levels of communication, you should be able to interact with people of all abilities and needs.

Chapter 9: Formal vs. Informal Communication

No matter the form of communication you are using, such as written or verbal, before engaging, you have to consider whether formal or informal communication is best. To put it simply, informal communication tends to have a free flow while formal communication is generally organized, and the channels of communication are generally predefined.

Think of advertising to better differentiate between the two. Watching a commercial or reading a billboard would be considered formal communication. The medium is direct and the message official and constant. Now, word-of-mouth would be an example of informal communication. This is where people essentially use a grapevine to talk about the merits of a product or service.

Overall the informal type is largely based on opinion, personal experience, and anecdotal evidence. However, the formal type is usually very reliable. It is based on evidence and the claims are backed up. For example, you are watching a commercial about a new car. The commercial will usually use both informal and formal communication. The formal would be offering statistics for things, such as the gas mileage. This has been tested and you can be assured that the numbers provided are accurate. The informal would be something along the lines of the company stating that the vehicle is the best for travelers, families or other types of drivers.

When looking at both types in a professional atmosphere, the formal type is considered to be the superior choice. The information is kept more secure and you do not have to worry about long chains of communication causing a distortion of the facts or primary points. It is a systematic and timely flow of information, making it the most effective choice. Now, informal can be efficient, albeit not as secure. The efficiency stems from coworkers being able to discuss issues related to work in a way that saves time.

There are four types of both formal and informal communication. With the formal type, these include:

- **Bottom-up or upward:** This describes the flow of communication starting with the most entry-level employees and then making its way up the chain to the company's most superior authority.

- **Lateral or horizontal:** When there are two coworkers at the same level, but in different departments, the communication between them is defined as lateral or horizontal.

- **Top down or upward:** This describes the company's highest authority sending communications down to those below them.

- **Diagonal or crosswise:** This describes the communication among two coworkers who work at different levels and in two different departments.

Examples of formal communication in the workplace include commands, reports, requests, and orders. All companies will have their own preferred methods and channels for delivering formal communication. However, most will use a type of hierarchal chain of command for this purpose. Overall, getting information to the right people as efficiently as possible without sacrificing the facts is the ultimate and most important goal.

The four types associated with the informal type include:

- **Cluster chain:** With this type, one person takes a few people they trust, and they give them information. These people then find people they trust and tell them. The chain continues.

- **Single strand chain:** This is what you might remember as being referred to as the game of telephone when you were younger. You tell someone something, they tell another who tells another, so on and so forth.

- **Gossip chain:** This is when an individual provides information to a group of people. Each member of the group tells another group of people, allowing the information to be widely distributed.

- **Probability chain:** A person takes a random coworker and gives them information. The information is not particularly important.

Examples of informal communication in the workplace include casual discussion, sharing of feelings and gossip. In most cases, the transmission of communication does not have any type of predefined channel. Information tends to be rapidly shared because it can flow in all directions freely and without any form of organization inhibiting it. This is a natural form of communication you will find in all workplaces. It is how coworkers can get to know each other and discuss matters that impact both their personal and professional lives.

Overall, it is important to master both of these forms of communication since both have their place. However, it is important that you use the right one at the right times. Make sure to always take into consideration the confidentiality of the correspondence and if it needs to be high, formal will be the way to go.

However, when you are simply looking to discuss basic matters and you need non-confidential information to be quickly spread, your best bet will be the informal route. As you perfect your advanced communication skills, you will start to just naturally choose the right one without even giving it much thought.

Chapter 10: Conflict Communication

Conflict happens, but when you are a skilled communicator, you are generally able to resolve it via communication alone. The first step is understanding the facts surrounding the conflict. For example, if you and your spouse are arguing about something, what started the argument? The next step is looking for a point of compromise.

You will also need to consider the environment and your relationship with the person you are having conflict with. There are different ways to approach conflict at work with a coworker than there is if you are having an argument with a lifelong friend.

Once all of the above is determined, the next step is to make sure that you are calm. You never want to discuss conflict when you are angry or upset. This will make it too difficult to use logic and proper conflict resolution. Take a short time to cool down and analyze the situation before attempting to resolve it.

When it comes to conflict communication, use your words in person. You want to be able to talk to the person face-to-face and use verbal communication. This will allow you to analyze their body language and really hear what they have to say.

Once the conversation starts, allow the other person to talk first. Utilize active listening to really hear what they are saying. Make sure to allow them to finish their thoughts before you provide yours. Once you both have made your thoughts and feelings clear, work to empathize. Most conflicts arise as a result of a misunderstanding of some sort. Now that you have both listened to each other, you can often find a common ground. This common ground is what you will use to resolve the conflict.

One of the most important elements of conflict communication is to put yourself second. Even if you fully believe you are right, remember that the other person does too. With empathy, a cool head, active listening and choosing your words wisely, you will find that most conflicts are not difficult to solve.

Conclusion

Thank you for making it through to the end of this book, let's hope it was informative and able to provide you with all of the tools you need to achieve your goals whatever they may be.

The next step is to evaluate your own communication skills. You learned a lot here, so give it a day to really sink in. From here, choose one chapter to start with. Verbal is likely the best place to get started since it is the most basic form of human communication. Explore the information presented here to ensure that your verbal communication is not only on par but as effective as you need them to be.

Once you master advanced verbal communication, the other forms will come easier to you. Look at the examples and relate them to your life and experiences. Think about how they have impacted your thoughts, as well as things like your propensity to purchase items you have seen in advertisements. When thinking about those that spurred a purchase, what was it about the advertisement that made you so excited about the product or service? Once you determine this, you can harness the persuasive communication technique yourself to persuade others and ensure that all forms of communication that you engage in are clear and articulate.

Communication is used for everything from catching up with a friend to getting to the top at work. With this book, you have the tools you need to soar to the most effective communication style possible.

Finally, if you found this book useful in any way, a review on Amazon is always appreciated!

CPSIA information can be obtained
at www.ICGtesting.com
Printed in the USA
BVHW091055090621
609091BV00009B/1053

9 791280 320445